WITHIN
THE CHANCEL

WITHIN THE CHANCEL

THOMAS A. STAFFORD

Illustrated by the Author

ABINGDON PRESS
NEW YORK • NASHVILLE

WITHIN THE CHANCEL

Library of Congress Catalog Card Number: 55-6766

SET UP, PRINTED, AND BOUND BY THE PARTHENON PRESS, AT NASHVILLE, TENNESSEE, UNITED STATES OF AMERICA

AD DEI GLORIAM

O send out thy light and thy truth: let them lead me; let them bring me unto thy holy hill, and to thy tabernacles. Then will I go unto the altar of God, unto God my exceeding joy.

—Ps. 43:3-4

Foreword

PROTESTANTS TODAY ARE SHOWING A RAPIDLY INCREASING INTEREST IN the beautification of God's house and the enrichment of worship. This is true even in the denominations which have a very simple liturgy. Many new churches are being built, and many old churches are being remodeled, to provide a chancel and central altar—or worship center, as some prefer to call it—either in the principal place of worship or in an adjoining chapel.

All this is a natural reaction from the severity of architecture and furnishings and the ultraplainness of worship during the period of Puritan ascendancy. But one can already observe in some cases an eagerness to decorate and elaborate overmuch. Paul not only counseled the early Christians about doing things "decently and in order." He also commended moderation. His counsel is still as valid as ever, and in no respect more than with reference to church equipment and adornment.

This manual is written from the viewpoint of aiming at such moderation, and it is not intended to favor any particular style of architecture, plan of ornamentation, or ecclesiastical fad. It is necessary to take a stand on some matters, however, and for practical as well as artistic reasons I am committed to the belief that the divided type of chancel, with a central altar or Communion table, contributes to reverent worship in the house of God. At the same time I firmly believe that vigorous preaching is a fundamental and indispensable requirement of an evangelical ministry, and that it must be constantly emphasized in keeping with the Protestant tradition. Regard for order and beauty ever needs to be matched by spiritual vitality.

To a considerable extent this is a companion to my earlier book *Christian Symbolism in the Evangelical Churches*, in which the chapter on "The Symbolism of a Church" attracted much attention and brought me many requests for information, especially regarding chancel arrangement. This book may answer some of those questions, but it is intended to be simply a brief, nontechnical manual. It does not go into the rites and ceremonies customarily performed in the chancel, nor into details of the equipment used in such. These matters differ among denominations, and can best be studied in denominational manuals. It is my hope that this book will serve as a simple guide to ministers and church members who are concerned to make and keep the chancel of the church a worthy center for the worship of God.

THOMAS A. STAFFORD

Acknowledgment is due to those who have supplied pictures of church and chapel chancels which appear in this book—especially to Eggers and Higgins, architects, New York City, for the picture of the chancel of the First Congregational Church, Columbus, Ohio; to G. J. Schanbacher and Son, interior decorators, Springfield, Illinois, for the picture of the chancel of the First Baptist Church, Kalamazoo, Michigan; and to Charles J. Betts, advisory architect of the Board of Church Extension of the Disciples of Christ, Indianapolis, Indiana, for the picture of the interior of the First Christian Church at Clinton, Illinois.

Special thanks are due to Edward F. Jansson, architect of the Interdenominational Bureau of Architecture, 740 Rush Street, Chicago, for assistance in obtaining pictures of various chancels.

Fred A. Hilgart, of Giannini and Hilgart, 1359 North Noble Street, Chicago, gave valuable help in the preparation of the chapter on stained glass.

The Morehouse-Gorham Company, New York City, graciously furnished much of the data concerning the flag of the Protestant Episcopal Church.

The National Council of the Churches of Christ in the United States of America supplied a copy of a resolution concerning the use of flags in churches.

To all these collaborators cordial thanks for their help and courtesy.

T. A. S.

Contents

List of Illustrations

Drawings

Photographs of Chancels

— I —

Beauty in God's House

IT IS NOTABLE THAT AS THE ARTISTIC POWERS OF A PEOPLE DEVELOP they tend to beautify the appurtenances of their worship. This observation is equally true of both ancient and modern times. With the remarkable spread of higher education in the last half century there has come a feeling for refinement in Protestant worship and more orderly administration of the sacraments. Congregations everywhere today are demanding the open chancel, with an altar or Communion table the focus of attention. This trend is observable in all the leading Protestant denominations, even in those which do not use a formal liturgy and which permit much ministerial freedom in the conduct of worship. Considering the prevailing state of opinion on such matters fifty years ago, the change is marvelous.

It is now generally accepted that there is no biblical justification for constructing a plain, ugly-looking church with an exterior not much different from a public hall and an interior completely devoid of either cultural or artistic effect. Today the young generation is keenly cognizant of the influence which a beautiful church exercises on mind and spirit. Young churchgoers, especially in the cities, tend either to make excuses for staying away from services in a very plain meetinghouse, or to attend some more attractive church; while some of the older folk stubbornly argue against making any concession to such moods, pleading that what was good enough for mother should be good enough for her grandchildren. Such intransigeance is becoming rarer every day, and many laymen and ministers are now eagerly seeking to obtain historical perspective in matters of worship and are gladly rediscovering the rich heritage of the past. They are not seeking a return to the uses and abuses of medieval times that provoked and made inevitable the Protestant Reformation, but are endeavoring to recover with enlightened discrimination the permanent liturgical values that make for dignity, beauty, order, and uplift in the services of God's house. They want the church to indicate to them that it is a very special place, unlike any other which they frequent in the course of their daily lives—a place that inevitably suggests, by its exterior and interior, worship, meditation, and the high significance of religion in life.

About half a century ago, especially in the middle-western and western states, there were a great many churches built according to the famous Akron plan, with a view to obtaining maximum seating and seeing capacity, regardless of acoustical excellence or aesthetic effect. The place of greatest importance in this frankly utilitarian hall of assembly was a platform with a central pulpit backed by three thronelike chairs, one for the officiating minister and, on occasion, the others for participants such as a visiting preacher or lecturer. Behind and above the platform area were the choir loft and the organ—with its great row of gilded pipes, including, perhaps, a number of dummies. In this conspicuous coign of vantage there was inevitable temptation for the choir or quartet to show off, more or less. The preacher could hardly avoid being conscious that he was the center of attention throughout the entire service of worship. The curved pews, set on a floor which sloped downward to the platform, afforded a stadium-like view of whatever was going on. The place was usually almost as devoid of religious symbolism as a Mohammedan mosque. The windows were filled with pictures of biblical scenes and imitations in stained glass of the popular religious paintings of Hofmann, Plockhorst, and others. To a sensitive mind the total effect was rather depressing, in spite of the fact that in many such churches there were eloquent preachers who would be hard to match today, and a warm, refreshing, spiritual fellowship that is still a blessed memory to many old-timers.

As long as artistic taste remained generally on the level of the commonplace, such church structures were easily tolerated, if not revered. However, with the rapidly increasing urbanization of the American people in the twentieth century and the multiplication of high schools and colleges throughout the country, a feeling for refinement and beauty developed that expressed itself in new types of house decoration and ingenious conveniences in keeping with the rapid advances being made in science and industry. Under such circumstances it was inevitable that the Akron-style churches should be regarded ultimately as "an-

Third Presbyterian Church, Rochester, New York

Akron-isms," as George Hedley humorously suggests in his book *Christian Worship*.

In recent decades the trend toward improvement and beautification of God's house has expressed itself mainly in two modes: (1) a return to the great church architecture of the past, particularly Gothic; and (2) use of modern, functional architecture, with emphasis on clean lines and elimination of costly structural appendages no longer desirable.

Undoubtedly, lovers of Gothic can make an impressive plea for the beauty and indefinable sense of uplift that it affords. However, its costliness, both in terms of building and maintenance, as well as the acoustical problem it usually involves, should all be considered very carefully before building in that style.

On the other hand, while the functional type of church building is relatively economical to construct and satisfies the modern desire for clean lines and effective use of all available space, it needs to be carefully planned by an architect who has a genuine feeling for church art, so that both exterior and interior will leave no doubt in the mind of the beholder that the structure has been specifically designed for a church rather than as a copy of an exposition building at a world's fair. Some of the new functional-type churches are beautiful and impressive so far as the interior, and especially the chancel, is concerned; but, on the outside, they might easily be mistaken for something else, if it were not for an oversize Latin cross in plain view.

In the functional type of church one sometimes sees pictures and carvings which are more or less consistent with the present-day cult of unintelligibility that obtains so much praise from certain high priests of the inner temples of art. To a person of plain common sense much ultramodern artistic expression is almost, if not altogether, devoid of rational meaning. It seems grotesque, abnormal, and unrelated to reality.

The story is told of a recently exhibited painting which was given profuse praise in a citation by an "expert." Afterward it was discovered that it was really a daub aimlessly done by a six-year-old child, and that it had been framed, given a cryptic title, and sent for exhibit by an adult. Some critic, with more imagination than good judgment, fell joyfully for the hoax.

Fortunately this queer artistic trend has had but a slight effect on the arts of the church. Fantastic and puzzling portrayals of figures of beings, human or divine, have no place in God's house, which should not have art-gallery features that make for the distraction of the worshipers. The beauty in God's house should be such as to penetrate the mind quietly, yet pervasively. Obvious overdecoration, complexity of symbolism, and vulgar display of any kind hinder devotion.

It is greatly significant that through the ages the noblest works of art have been consecrated to the adornment of temples and churches, and this remains true even in our materialistic age.

— II —

Worship and Architecture

PRIMITIVE CHRISTIAN WORSHIP CONSISTED OF TWO MAIN ELEMENTS—the sacramental and the prophetic. We are told that the early Christians "continued steadfastly in the apostles' doctrine and fellowship, and in breaking of bread, and in prayers."

The "breaking of bread" began in a table-fellowship. A first-century sacramental service was a kind of intimate, homelike luncheon served in a dwelling house. It was a meeting of a few Christian friends for the purpose of symbolic breaking of bread with thanksgiving to God for Christ's atoning death, and for remembrance of Christ as he indicated at the Last Supper. Among the early Roman Christians this symbolic luncheon was called a sacrament, a term derived from the *sacramentum*—the oath of loyalty taken by a Roman soldier. However, the Christians pledged their fealty to Jesus Christ.

By preaching, these early Christians encouraged one another in witnessing for the faith in an uncongenial environment, and sought to win converts. Thus the sacramental and the prophetic were complementary at the very beginning, and it is one of the tragedies of Christian history that they were ever separated and placed in opposition to each other. "For as often as ye eat this bread, and drink this cup, ye do shew the Lord's death till he come" is both a sacramental and a prophetic declaration.

Until the middle of the third century the Communion was administered on a movable wooden table. The language of Rev. 6:9, "I saw under the altar the souls of them that were slain for the word of God," may have inspired the third-century papal decree that the Communion be celebrated "above the tombs of martyrs," which probably led to the Roman Catholic practice of placing relics in tomblike altars made of stone. The Council of Epaone, France, in A.D. 517, decreed that no altar should be consecrated thereafter with chrism (consecrated oil) unless constructed of stone.

In the primitive church the Communion table was so arranged that it could be surrounded on all sides by communicants. In the Middle Ages the altar was placed against the liturgical-east wall of the church so as to prevent all access from that side. (The liturgical east is the location of the altar, not necessarily or always the true east.)

Until the Christian religion was officially recognized by a decree of Emperor Constantine in A.D. 313, it exercised no significant architectural influence. Prior to that time some church edifices were built, because it is recorded that a number of them were destroyed by Emperor Diocletian. These earliest Christian churches were probably built somewhat like the Roman *schola*, or small meeting hall, used by pagan social groups for their functions. However, the use of such structures seems to have made no lasting mark on either architecture or worship.

As soon as persecution ceased and the Christians came out of hiding, general need for public places of worship arose. Obviously, the Christians did not want to use or copy the temples that had fallen into disuse because of the decadence of pagan religions. Instead they were attracted to the basilican type of buildings commonly used as courts of justice and halls of assembly. They found them easily transformable into commodious places of worship.

The Roman basilican type was simple and economical to build. It was rectangular, divided lengthwise by rows of columns. Adapted for church use, it had a semicircular apse at one end of the principal room, the nave, and at the opposite end an arcaded entrance, or narthex, which extended the full width of the building. In some cases there was an apse at both ends of the nave. In the center was an atrium, or courtyard, with a fountain for ablutions—a feature evidently borrowed from spacious Roman dwelling houses of that period. Later it disappeared from the churches, but the holy-water font at the entrance of Roman Catholic churches today may be a survival of an idea derived from its prototype, the fountain in the atrium.

In the basilican type of church the altar was placed immediately in front of the apse. In many cases, because of the smallness of the apse, the choir and minor clergy were placed in front of the altar, in the body of the nave, in an enclosed rectangular space surrounded by a railing. An ambo, or pulpit, was placed on each side of this reserved space. Doubtless this arrangement was the prototype of the placement of pulpit and lectern in the chancels of later times. In the churches of the basilican type the part of the nave not occupied by the choir was reserved for baptized full members of the church who were seated by placing the men on one side and the women on the other. Worshipers who were not members were permitted to stand in the narthex or atrium. Until the fifth century the priest faced the congregation while officiating at the altar. After the fifth century the congregation as well as the priest faced the apse, looking toward the liturgical east—the place where the altar stood, irrespective of orientation.

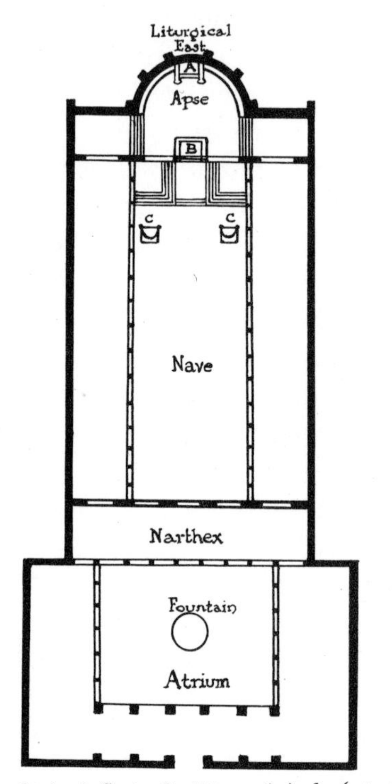

A - Bishop's Seat; B - Altar; C - Ambo (pulpit)

PLAN OF EARLY CHRISTIAN BASILICA

In early Christian architecture, especially in the Near East, a good many churches were constructed on a circular plan, with a dome supported by an inner rotunda of columns or an octagon. In some cases the dome stood on four piers, with apselike structures on each of the four sides.

Byzantine architecture represents a combination of the classical with an elaboration of the domical style. The typical Byzantine dome was erected on four arches enclosing a square. A cruciform church building topped by a Byzantine dome combined the chief symbol of the Christian faith with the emotional lift which a large dome inspires.

The Byzantine influence in church art and architecture was extensive and continued in the West down to the fourteenth century. It was felt particularly in Italy at Venice and Ravenna in the pre-Romanesque period, prior to A.D. 800, during which there was more or less fusion of Eastern and Western ideas of church building. However, in this period,

The Grosse Pointe Memorial Church, Grosse Pointe Farms, Michigan

owing to greatly disturbed economic and political conditions, church architecture in the West made very little progress outside Italy. Russian church architecture from the tenth century to modern times is typically Byzantine. However, Russian domes were constructed with a bulbous shape in order, it is said, more readily to throw off heavy winter snows. This type dome may be seen on Russian Orthodox churches in America.

Byzantine architects and artists produced some of the most beautiful churches which remain as examples of early Christian architecture, notably the magnificent church known as Sancta Sophia in Constantinople and the lovely church of San Marco in Venice, which contains some of the finest mosaic extant. In the construction and decoration of apses, domes, and altars, Byzantine builders and artists were superbly skillful and ingenious. They attained magnificence, but generally sought to subordinate it to sublimity.

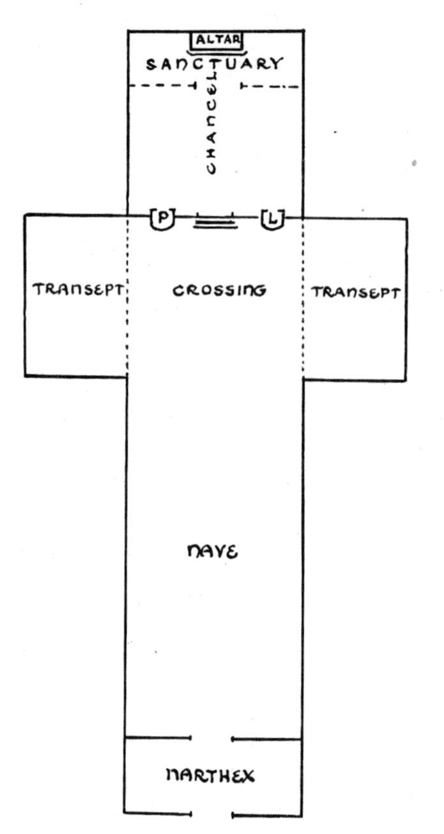

CRUCIFORM PLAN

In the Romanesque stage of architectural development, which was mainly characterized by the round arch and vault type of structure, with piers instead of columns, the conversion of the basilican church plan to a cruciform shape by construction of transepts and a crossing at right angles to the greatest length of the church, between the nave and the apse, introduced a feature characteristic of this style. However, it should be noted that some of the early Christian basilicas had a cross-like form.

An important modification of Romanesque architecture resulted from the introduction of spacious domes modeled after the Byzantine style. This vaulted type of construction afforded large unbroken expanses of ceiling and wall suitable for brilliant decoration with paintings and mosaic, especially in the apse, where the altar stood.

Romanesque development of the basilican style determined largely the basic plan of the great churches and cathedrals of the West in medieval times.

The Gothic style of church architecture, which originated in France in the twelfth century, is mainly characterized by a distinctive method of distributing weights and stresses on slender, upright piers with counter-balancing buttresses, also by the pointed arch. Gothic developed out of the Romanesque style, in which lateral thrust on the walls, due to the weight of the roof, was counterbalanced by massive masonry. The Gothic ground plan does not differ radically from that of the Roman basilican type. However, in general appearance, both exterior and interior, the great medieval Gothic churches and cathedrals were vastly different from the Christian churches built in the reign of Emperor Constantine. Most of them were decorated with an immense amount of delicate tracery and a multiplicity of representations drawn not only from human activities but also from the whole realm of nature. In some of the most magnificent cathedrals hardly any space was left bare of ornament. The effect is overwhelming. Such ornate structures are the architectural opposites of the stately Greek temples and Roman basilicas of earlier times in which beauty, strength, and symmetry were achieved with restrained use of ornamentation.

In the main, typical Renaissance church architecture, which developed three regional styles, closely resembles the Gothic style and generally exhibits the same flair for ornamentation and elaborate detail, although Renaissance church architecture in its purest form indicates a return to Greek and Roman architecture of the classical period. Such variations in architectural taste had corresponding effects on church interiors, and especially on the decoration of the chancel and its equipment. In the Middle Ages the general trend was toward enrichment and excessive ornamentation.

In large measure the enlightenment of the Renaissance period prepared the way for the Protestant Reformation, which made important changes in church architecture concomitantly with the reform of faith and order.

In the great medieval Gothic cathedrals and churches of Europe, with magnificent chancels, long naves, and very high ceilings, it is evident that the main purpose in building them was to provide a proper setting for elaborate rites, ceremonies, and processionals. Most of them had no pulpit, because there was little or no preaching. The congregation was expected to stand during the services, thus making seating arrangements unnecessary as well as providing larger capacity to handle crowds. The Mass was the usual form of worship, and it was often badly recited in Latin by inadequately educated priests. The congregations were mostly illiterate and, therefore, uncritical. Seldom was preaching heard, and then only by a bishop or some other church dignitary on a special occasion.

The Protestant Reformation magnified the pulpit. The translation of the Bible into the language of the common people caused churchmen to demand that it be read and explained in church; and, therefore, preaching, which had long been neglected, became an important part of religious services in the reformed churches.

The revulsion against Roman Catholic abuses was so strong as to cause the reformers to strip the churches of much of the paraphernalia used in connection with the celebration of the Mass, after it was rejected as the typical form of corporate worship. There was a period following the Reformation in which fanatical iconoclasm destroyed many architectural and artistic treasures that would now be cherished and preserved by Protestants in a quieter and more reasonable mood.

The Puritan reaction in the Anglican Church, the Evangelical Revival in England, and the polity of the various English nonconformist churches, all tended to emphasize bareness in the sanctuary, with the pulpit centered and high, and no sign of an altar, except, perhaps, a Communion table.

On the continent of Europe the Lutherans retained the chancel and altar in their churches, as well as a distinctly liturgical form of worship. It should also be noted that the Moravians retained a rich liturgy.

It is said that John Calvin used to conduct somewhat formal church services behind a Communion table, going only to the pulpit to preach.

John Wesley and John Calvin were both liturgists, but their post-mortem influence in this respect was of short duration.

After his death Wesley's followers soon abandoned all pretense of retaining his abbreviation of the Anglican liturgy; and, in common with Presbyterians, Baptists, and Congregationalists, they worshiped God in meetinghouses, which were generally constructed somewhat like a public hall, with a pulpit or rostrum on the center of the platform. All this was quite natural in a period when stirring pulpit oratory and strong religious emotion were held in high esteem by the common people.

Until the beginning of the twentieth century, bareness and lack of any ecclesiastical equipment were quite characteristic of most non-liturgical churches in America.

As noted previously, the altar was one of the many structures of the church which suffered during the Reformation. Before the reaction occasioned by the Reformation, however, the altar, in the process of architectural development, became quite elaborate; and in the pre-Reformation period, Gothic churches and cathedrals attained magnificent proportions and decorations in conformity with the splendor of the Gothic style.

After the Reformation in England, and before the restorative ritual reforms introduced by Archbishop Laud, many parish churches which had removed the stone altars had a long table placed in the nave, so that the congregation might gather round it and partake of Holy Communion in the style of the primitive church. The dominant idea in the rubrics of the pre-Laudian *Book of Common Prayer* was to bring priest and people together in corporate worship.

Because of sacerdotal connotations the Puritan opposition to the word "altar" was so strong that it was expunged from the *Book of Common Prayer* and "God's board" or "the table" substituted wherever the word "altar" occurred. In the course of time this extreme attitude gradually changed, and the words "altar" and "table" came to be used interchangeably.

ALTAR SIMPLICITY

The re-establishment of the altar, which we are witnessing so commonly today, enhances the impressiveness of the Communion service, dignifies the sacred wedding ceremony, and sheds over every office and ritual of the church an influence rich in significance.

The reasons for re-establishing chancel and altar are not only artistic and practical; as regards desire for liturgical improvements, they are deeply rooted in the cultivation of spiritual responses and a sense of reverence for God's house, which is everywhere taught in both Old and New Testaments. Jesus reverenced the temple and called it his Father's house. So far as we know, he never said a word disparagingly about it. In his time it certainly was not a plain, unattractive structure, but a very spacious and ornate edifice of astounding beauty and rich in symbolical significance.[1]

It is well, also, to recall the word of the Lord about Zion which was delivered to the prophet Isaiah: "The glory of Lebanon shall come unto thee, the fir tree, the pine tree, and the box together, to beautify the place of my sanctuary; and I will make the place of my feet glorious" (60:13).

An unknown poet of the sixteenth century wrote the following lines:

> 'Tis only base, niggard heresy
> To think Religion loves deformity.
> Glory did never yet make God the less,
> Neither can beauty defile holiness.
> What's more magnificent than heaven, yet where
> Is there more love and piety than there?

If the church is to be the place where the presence of God is spiritually experienced in company with his people, it should by its beauty and comeliness reflect the high honor we desire to pay to that presence; it should be a place where we instinctively lower our voices and sense an indefinable atmosphere in which things invisible penetrate our being and elevate our thoughts for a while above "the madding crowd's ignoble strife."

[1] The stoa basilica of Herod's Temple, built about 18 B.C., had 162 Corinthian columns of white marble.

— III —

The Chancel

WE LEARN FROM EUSEBIUS IN THE FOURTH CENTURY THAT IN THE EARLY Christian churches there were low screens, or cancelli, surrounding the altar on all sides.

The Latin word *cancelli* has reference to a latticework screen. The English word "chancel" is used with reference to the space in a church which is reserved for the officiating clergy and which is generally separated from the rest of the church floor space by a railing or screen.

In the secular Roman basilicas, which were prototypes of the early Christian church buildings in the Roman Empire, the chancel was the space railed off to separate the judges and council from the audience.

In present-day usage the word "chancel" refers specifically to the part of the church used by the ministrants in worship and commonly separated from the remainder of the floor space of the church by a screen or rail, usually open at the center for access.

In some Protestant churches the word "chancel" is used with reference to a space railed off in front of the pulpit.

The floor of the chancel should be several feet higher than the level of the nave, in order that the altar may be fully visible to the entire congregation from a level floor. The number of steps at the place of entry in the center is a matter of choice, two or three being most common, perhaps.

In early Christian churches the chancel was usually small. When choirs began to be seated in chancels, the length was extended and the entire enclosed space came to be known as "the choir," a term still more or less in use in England.

Commonly, in liturgical churches, the altar with its appurtenances, the organ, and the seats for the choir and clergy are placed within the chancel, which is divided so as to provide an open way from a central aisle to the steps of the altar, and also to permit seating the choir in two sections facing each other, instead of looking toward the congregation. Praise should be directed toward the altar. A church should not copy a theater or music hall in any respect. There should be no exhibitionism on the part of anyone leading or assisting in worship.

A great merit of the divided chancel is that it does not encourage exhibitionism. Moreover, it is functionally adaptable to a variety of conditions, ranging all the way from low-church simplicity to a high degree of formalism. It is an encouragement to reverence, which is greatly to be desired in any church.

For the sake of acoustical advantage pulpit and lectern are usually located at the meeting of chancel and nave. Location of a pulpit is purely a matter of favorable acoustics and can be best settled by a skilled architect. Whichever side is chosen for the pulpit, the lectern, of course, will be placed on the opposite side.

In the Protestant tradition the pulpit is a symbol of the importance of the preaching of the Word of God. After the Reformation the pulpit became the most important piece of church furniture. It was usually built in polygonal form and was the object of much fine craftsmanship. Modern Protestant pulpits are usually less prominent and of simpler design. Whatever the design, it should be in harmony with the surroundings; and care should be taken to see that it is not undersized in proportion to the total area of the chancel. It may have carved on it symbols of the evangelists or figures representing great preachers—like Savonarola, Luther, Calvin, Wesley—or some of the most important Christian symbols or monograms that would be appropriate. If there are steps leading up to the pulpit, they should be few in number and broad enough to keep a guest preacher or anyone unfamiliar with the approach from stumbling on them. In Gothic style churches it may be necessary to have a canopy above the pulpit, even when there is a public-address system available, because sometimes the latter device fails to function properly, to the discomfort of all concerned. Otherwise, the great amount of vacant space aloft may waste the utterances of the preacher and make hearing difficult, if not impossible. This is a common fault in Gothic churches. In any case, in such a church it is important to speak slowly enough so that each syllable of a word is distinctly pronounced—a good

Courtesy of William Wollin Studio

GRACE EPISCOPAL CHURCH, Madison, Wisconsin

rule in any type of church. Also, advice of a competent acoustical engineer may help greatly to solve the hearing problem.

A lectern, or reading desk, should be substantial looking and in keeping with the pulpit. The extremely narrow kind, whether made of metal or wood, should be avoided. The kind that can be turned around has no special utility in the average church and is not worth the extra cost.

In the usual type of divided chancel the choir is seated on both sides of the approach to the altar. In such cases, if the organist also serves as choirmaster, it is necessary to place a mirror on the wall opposite the console of the organ in order that the section of the choir which faces the side opposite the organ may see the directing motions of the organist's hand. If there is a choirmaster, he should never stand in front of the altar when conducting the singing.

In some liturgical churches the organist and choir are placed in a balcony at the back of the church, or elsewhere outside the chancel. In churches of recent construction the organ is generally designed to be heard rather than seen. The eye-distracting, old-fashioned array of organ pipes, once so popular, is now generally regarded with strong disfavor.

Good pipe organs are expensive, generally require maintenance, take up a lot of room, and need to be protected from extremes of temperature and humidity. Nevertheless, if it can be afforded, a pipe organ is preferable to any other. However, in many small or medium-sized churches in which economy is an important desideratum, an electronic instrument of the less expensive type, which has a distinctive tone as compared with a pipe organ, may serve well enough and require a relatively small outlay. The higher-priced electronic organs can be played so as to produce quite realistic pipe-organ effects.

The dominant position within the chancel is occupied by the altar, in the area known as the sanctuary. The word "sanctuary" is commonly used in nonliturgical churches in America with reference to the part of the church plant where religious services are held, as distinguished from the part used for other purposes. However, in the strict sense the sanctuary is the most sacred part of the church structure, where the altar is situated in the liturgical east and which, in many cases, is separated from the rest of the chancel by a railing. As the etymology of the word "sanctuary" suggests, it is *the holy place*. Its prototype is the Holy of Holies of the Jewish temple.

The altar itself may be used (as it is in many Presbyterian churches) for a Communion table; if it is not, it is customary to have in the front of the nave tables covered with white linen cloths, upon which are placed the vessels and elements which are used in administration of Holy Communion. Some churches have a sort of self-service arrangement attached at the back of the Communion rail for the sake of saving time when there is a large number to be served. The effect seems mechanical and uninspiring, unless managed with due regard for the solemnity of the occasion. I once attended a service of Holy Communion in a large church where eleven hundred persons participated in this fashion. All that the officiating minister said at each table was, "Kneel!" and "Rise!" The effect was startling.

In connection with the administration of Holy Communion it may be of passing interest to some readers to mention and briefly describe the following articles commonly used in liturgical churches:

CORPORAL—The linen cloth used upon the altar at Holy Communion.
PALL OR VEIL—A linen cover for the chalice.
LAVABO—A bowl used for washing the officiant's hands during celebration.
BURSE—A case for the corporal.
AMPULLA OR CRUET—A receptacle for wine or for water mixed with wine.
PYX—A covered receptacle for the elements.
PURIFICATOR—The small linen cloth used to cleanse the rim of the chalice during administration.

The above-described articles are not required for the great majority of Protestant churches, in which the sacrament of Holy Communion is now administered hygienically from individual Communion cups. This departure from ancient use is a step forward in keeping with modern medical research. Nevertheless, the chalice, with its ancient and holy associations, will forever remain as a precious symbol in Christian churches.

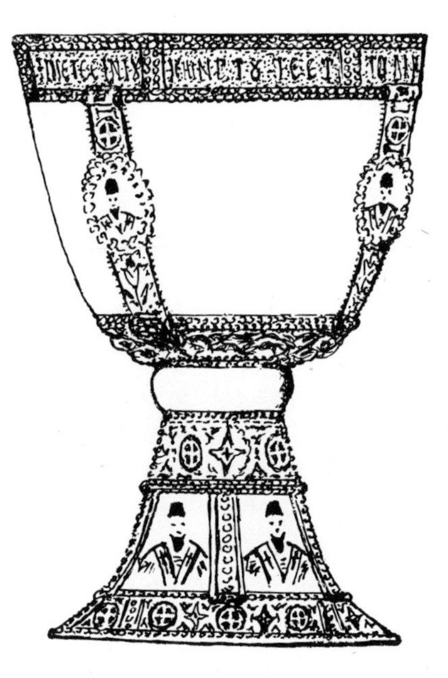

CHALICE, 11TH CENTURY

It is well for the church to possess

a removable, double-width *prie-dieu*, or kneeling bench, for use in front of the altar at weddings.

For sacramental purposes a baptismal font is an important part of the equipment of a church. Baptismal fonts have been used in Christian churches from ancient times. In the early churches, which during the period of persecution were mostly dwelling houses, fonts were simple metal vessels to hold water for baptism by infusion (pouring water on the head of the person being baptized) or by aspersion (sprinkling). Baptism by immersion, which many believe was the primitive form of the rite, became common after persecution ceased and churches could be built. The baptistery was often built as a separate structure near the church. A good many of the early baptisteries contained a font rather than a tank. However, few, if any, fonts now exist that were constructed before the eleventh century. The oldest fonts were simply cylindrical bowls of stone, generally supported by a single unadorned pillar. In the Middle Ages hexagonal and octagonal bowls were introduced. Many of them were elaborately decorated with sculpture and relief depicting scenes related to baptism or Christian symbols and monograms. In the thirteenth century lids came into use, and it is believed that their original purpose was to prevent sorcery. Some of these lids were very large, usually pyramidal in form and decorated elaborately.

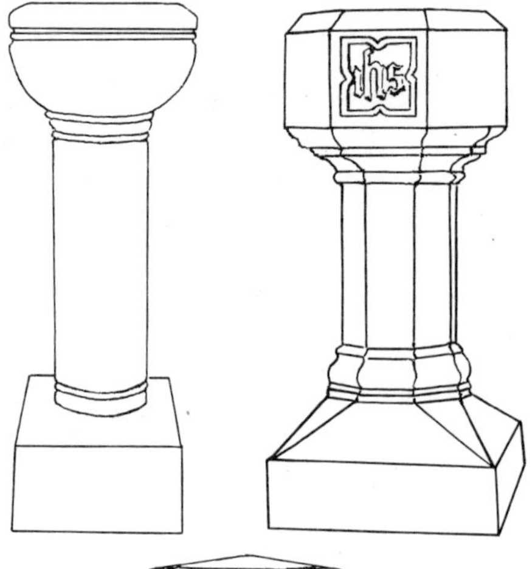

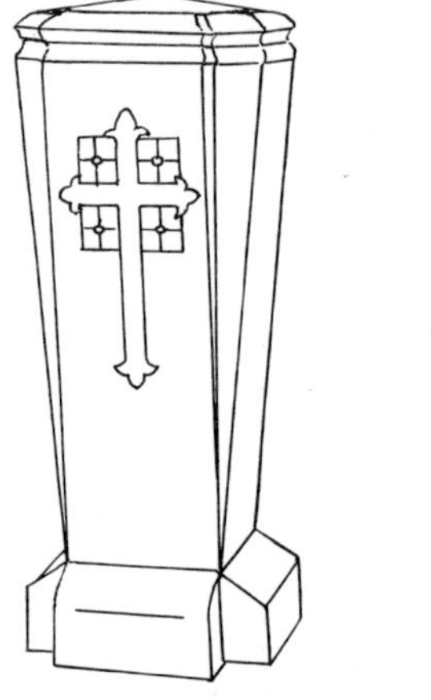

Types of Fonts

A baptismal font is usually made of stone, with the top hollowed to form a basin. Unless the basin is constructed so that it is connected with a drainpipe, a removable vessel of the proper shape and size should be inserted. When not in use, this vessel can be removed. When a font is not in use, it should, for the sake of cleanliness, be covered with a suitable lid.

Symbolism appearing on a font should be in harmony with the character of the chancel. A descending dove, representing the Holy Spirit, or the *IHS* monogram is always suitable.

An elaborate font in front of a simple and dignified chancel seems out of place.

According to tradition the proper place for the baptismal font was near the entrance to the nave of the church, so that it might serve as a symbol that baptism signifies entrance upon the Christian way of life. However, the desire of the congregations to see baptism administered ultimately caused the font to be placed in the chancel end of the church. This is the modern practice. It is seldom that one sees a baptismal font actually within the chancel area, as it is likely to be in the way when not in use.

A small shelf or stand at a convenient height near the font provides a handy place on which the minister can lay his service book while he is baptizing. It can also hold a towel with which he can dry his hands before picking up the book to complete the ritual. After the service of baptism the water should be poured on the ground outside the church, never into a drain.

In remodeling a chancel it would be well, if feasible, to remove from the walls, and place elsewhere, all memorial brass plaques, marble tablets, and symbolic devices that would not be in keeping with the purpose of the chancel and its proper symbolism.

— IV —

The Altar

THE ALTAR IS THE FOCUS OF THE WORSHIPERS' ATTENTION AND NEEDS TO be such, in itself and in its setting, so that it will arouse and maintain the spirit of reverent worship.

In nearly all churches which have an altar at the east wall, either a reredos or a dossal is provided to give a suitable setting for the altar. A reredos is a solid background, usually constructed of wood or stone and carved with suitable figures, monograms, or symbols. A dossal is a hanging cloth of good quality and heavy texture, generally red in color. The exact shade should be carefully chosen to harmonize with the surroundings and especially with the carpet which reaches from the steps of the chancel to the steps of the altar.

Sometimes the question is raised as to whether a small temporary reredos or short dossal might be fittingly used back of a Communion table with a cross and candles situated in front of a center pulpit and within the Communion rail. This arrangement, which may be intended to obscure partially the center pulpit and give somewhat the effect of an altar as a worship center, is certainly not ideal, because the minister still looks down over the cross when he is addressing the congregation. At best it is a makeshift, transitional step toward remodeling that part of the church as soon as it can be afforded.

When erecting an altar or providing for a Communion table for use at the highest level at the back, or east end, of the chancel, care should be taken to have it look large enough to be dominant. In large churches a chancel may be put off balance easily by having the altar too small or hidden from part of the congregation by some obstruction.

Frequently one sees a gradin, or shelf, rising from the floor behind and above an altar. It affords a convenient place for the altar cross and candlesticks and, if well designed, enhances the appearance of the altar.

Washington Park Methodist Church, Providence, Rhode Island

In the best Protestant tradition an altar is not regarded as a kind of stand or dresser to be decorated for show. As a rule the fewer and simpler its ornaments, in excess of a cross and two candlesticks, the better.

Altar with Gradin and Dossal

Commonly there are three covering cloths on a properly vested altar. These are listed here in the order of vesting: (1) a heavy linen cloth (usually waxed to make it resistant to dampness and therefore known as a cerecloth) the exact size of the mensa of the altar or top of the Communion table; (2) a cloth the exact size of the mensa with a superfrontal attached and hanging several inches over the front of the altar; (3) a white "fair linen cloth," the altar cloth proper, as wide as the mensa or table top, covering it entirely and hanging down over the ends of the altar almost to the floor.

If the altar is out from the wall and is used as a Communion table, it may be desirable to have the equivalent of the superfrontal at the back. This is a matter of choice. Or, in such cases the cloth with the superfrontal attached may be removed during a service of Holy Communion. A good many freestanding altars are ordinarily left without a covering.

An altar should be properly proportioned in width and height to the chancel in which it will occupy the place of highest honor. This is primarily an architect's problem. If steps are placed before the altar, they should be such as to afford safe standing room. Recently, while attending service in a beautiful Presbyterian church with a divided chancel which has an altar and three altar steps, I saw a visiting clergyman, after placing the filled collection plates on the altar, suddenly turn round and fall rather awkwardly forward because the steps were too narrow.

It is now customary, even in nonliturgical churches, to place a cross and two candlesticks upon an altar or Communion table. The cross is a symbol that transcends all isms.

An empty cross on an altar symbolizes the risen and ascended Christ. Very rarely one sees a crucifix (cross with a figure of Christ upon it) in a Protestant church, because that kind of realistic portrayal of the figure of Christ dying in agony on a cross is not favored. Christ overcame death —a fact signified by the empty cross.

It is quite fitting to have the letters *IHS* on an altar cross. They are usually taken as the first two and last letters of the word "Jesus" in Greek, but they are also the first three letters. A cross with these letters on it is not merely a cross; it is positively identified as representing the cross of Christ, the divine Saviour.

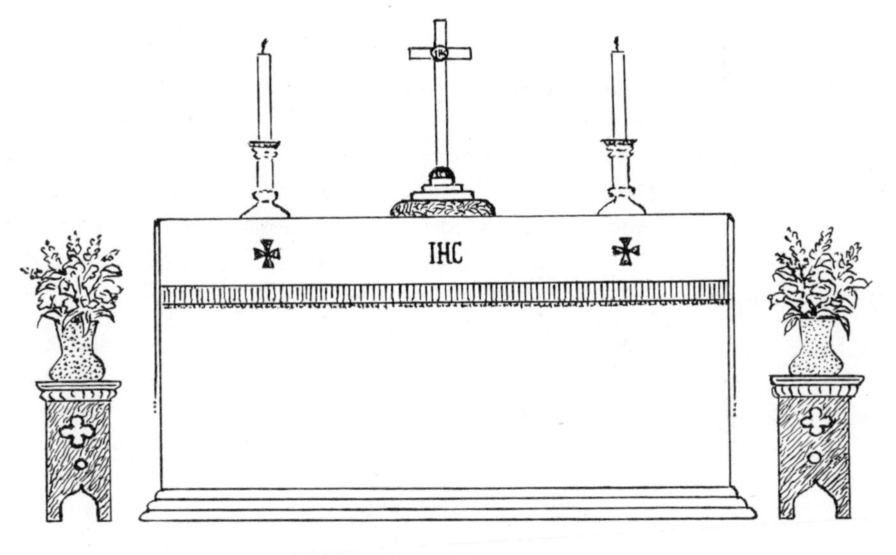

THE CROSS DOMINANT

It is important that a cross be properly proportioned to its surroundings. A small cross in a large chancel fails of impressiveness. But a cross disproportionately large is equally objectionable. If there is a high reredos or dossal back of the altar, the cross should be relatively tall and slender. Ideally the transverse member of a Latin cross should measure five-eighths the length of the upright member. Before any cross is purchased, cardboard models of various sizes should be put in the desired place on the altar and tested as to goodness of fit when viewed from the farthest back pews in the nave of the church. In this way a proper idea of the most desirable size can be determined.

Sometimes a skillful local woodworker can be employed to make a wooden cross and candlesticks with remarkably good effect. In California I have seen very beautiful crosses and candlesticks that were made by a local craftsman. They were made of carved wood overlaid with gold leaf; the carving was done so as to leave a somewhat uneven surface which reflected candlelight with extraordinary brilliance. Crosses made of wood are coming into favor, and why not? Christ was not crucified on a metal cross.

If a cross of wood is chosen and the background is a reredos of wood, the color of the cross should be enough different from the prevailing color of the reredos so that the cross can be seen distinctly when viewed from the rear of the nave.

Whatever the kind of cross chosen, it should be high enough so that the altar candles at their greatest height do not rise much, if any, above the crosspiece of the cross.

Vases containing flowers may be placed on the altar or gradin, although it seems preferable to have them on small tables at the side of the altar. Empty vases and empty collection plates should not be placed on the altar at any time. It may be desirable to place the filled collection plates on a small side table also.

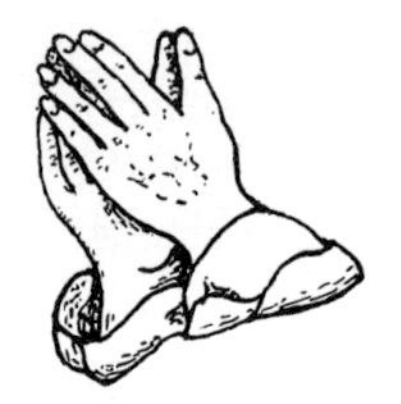

—V—

Symbolic Lights

AT PRESENT IN PROTESTANT CHURCHES THERE IS GREAT DIVERSITY AND some confusion in the use of symbolic lights.

As the altar cross is the central symbol in a Christian church, it should be high enough so that altar candles, at their greatest height, do not rise above the top of the cross. One frequently sees an altar cross dwarfed by tall candles; the effect is not pleasing to the eye.

THE CROSS DWARFED

The number of candles to be used on an altar or Communion table is a matter of choice.[1] In the ordinary evangelical church two candles on the altar are quite enough; but if the altar or table is wide, more may be desired. Too many candles make the sanctuary look showy, whereas simplicity should rule. I have a newspaper picture of a church decorated with a great array of Easter lilies and several thousand candles—one hesitates to quote the number mentioned beneath the picture. Only those who love display would be impressed by such a lavish decorative effect.

The disadvantage of too many lighted candles in the chancel is that some people in the congregation may find so much light, on or near the level of the eye, disturbing and objectionable, especially if there is

[1] Sir J. N. Comper, distinguished English church architect, says that two lights only upon the altar and never more than two is the use of the Anglican Church today and was the common use in pre-Reformation churches until the thirteenth century.

a draft which causes flickering. Moreover, beeswax candles of good quality are expensive.

The symbolism of altar candles is somewhat complex and unsettled, which may explain why one hears so many differing interpretations of various arrangements. The following notes on this subject give the generally accepted significance.

A three-branch light symbolizes the holy Trinity. A five-branch light symbolizes the five wounds in the body of our Lord. On the altars of the distinctively liturgical churches one frequently sees six lights. This number is said to signify that Christ died at the sixth day and hour. In Roman Catholic churches a seven-branch candlestick signifies the seven Catholic sacraments, whereas in Protestant churches it is generally regarded as signifying the seven gifts of the Holy Spirit. In passing, it should be said that the Menorah, or typical seven-branch candlestick used in Jewish temples and synagogues, seems somewhat out of place in a Christian church.

Two large candles standing, one to the right and the other to the left of the altar, in candlesticks set on the floor or on the altar, to the right and left of the cross, are called "eucharistic lights." They signify the divine and human natures of Christ. They are lighted when the sacrament of Holy Communion is being administered in liturgical churches. In other churches such candles are customarily lighted at every service of worship. The branched lights on the mensa of the altar, if such are used, are generally referred to as "office lights." They are properly used at nonsacramental services, or offices, and are commonly supposed to represent some fact in connection with the life or death of Jesus. Very rarely one sees four candles on an altar. They may be interpreted to mean that the life of Christ and his teachings are found in the four Gospels—Matthew, Mark, Luke, and John.

It is best to light candles with a lighting taper mounted on an instrument commonly called a "bell," which serves also as an extinguisher. In many churches in which formality is kept to a minimum the candles are lighted by someone appointed to do so before the congregation assembles, and are extinguished after it departs. In such cases the lighting should be done early enough so that no worshipers will have arrived. Once I arrived at a church only ten minutes before the morning service and, with other early arrivals, watched the janitor strut up the central aisle to the altar and light the candles with his cigarette lighter. The sight

Courtesy of The Gaddis Photography

First Methodist Church, Des Plaines, Illinois

was not conducive to reverence. On the other hand, lighting altar candles after the congregation is assembled can be made an impressive and beautiful prelude to the service of worship.

When there are a number of candles on the altar or Communion table, it is customary to light them beginning from one side with the candle farthest from the cross and moving up to the center, then beginning again from the outside candle on the other side. Extinguishing is then done in reverse order from the lighting. In liturgical churches the acolyte usually begins lighting on the "Epistle" side (the right as the congregation faces the altar) so that the last candle to be lit—and the first to be extinguished—is the candle nearest the cross on the "Gospel" (left) side. However, Percy Dearmer, an Anglican authority on liturgy, says that the order of lighting and extinguishing doesn't matter.

Sometimes one sees an altar or Communion table with a Bible, set on a sloping stand, at the center and an unlighted candle on either side of the Bible. Above the Bible there may be a suspended cross, and back of the Bible, on a fairly high retable, a chalice. Perhaps such an arrangement or combination is not very desirable, because the empty chalice, unused Bible, and unlighted candles seem to be without function. However, there is Anglican precedent for the placing of a Bible instead of a cross on the altar.

Before leaving the subject of symbolic lights in the chancel, a word of caution is necessary. A suspended sanctuary lamp kept continually lighted above the center of the chancel, in front of the altar or Communion table, is frequently called by Protestants an "everlasting light." It is not a fitting Protestant symbol, because in Roman Catholic churches it indicates that the "reserved" body and blood of Christ are within the tabernacle on the altar, and that, therefore, he is present in a physical or, perhaps better say, metaphysical sense. Sometimes Protestants give the explanation that the ever-burning light represents the everlasting Word of God. However, in order to avoid confusion it is best to omit this item of chancel furnishing; because by traditional usage it stands for the doctrine of transubstantiation, which Protestants reject.

— VI —

Monograms and Symbols

People have their minds so crowded perforce with secular images and symbols in the present workaday world, it has become more important than ever to surround them in church with some objective symbols pointing to the concerns of the spiritual life. Such symbols help to interrupt the worldly train of thought which is all too apt to occupy one's mind when one passes over the threshold of the church on the Lord's Day. It is notable that many modern philosophers are now taking overdue cognizance of the great importance of symbolism, not only in religion, but also in all human thought, speech, and action. Symbolism is now recognized as fundamentally related to the progress of human culture in all its aspects.

Monograms and symbols constitute the sign language of the church. The Chinese have a saying to the effect that a picture is worth ten thousand words. This is also true of Christian symbols. They are silent sermonets, endlessly fascinating to those who will lend attention. When properly understood, Christian monograms and symbols convey a wealth of meaning with a minimum of expression. So it was in the early church, and so it is today.

Use of them and instruction about them is to be commended. However, if there are a great many of them in the windows of the chancel or elsewhere in the church, or if they are too complicated for ready understanding, that is a fault, if not an abuse.

As the chancel contains the worship center of the church, the symbols of divinity naturally predominate in that location.

In case of remodeling or erection of a new church building the symbols should be chosen with great care, especially those which are to be in the chancel in full view of the entire congregation.

The following selection contains most of the monograms and symbols which are commonly chosen for the chancel; and it may, therefore, serve as a useful guide.[1] Opposite each illustration is a brief explanation.

This important literary symbol is generally used in the chancel, principally on the altar. It is shown in two forms; the first is that most commonly used. It also appears in capitals as *IHS* or *IHC*. Whatever the form, it is a contraction of the Greek word for "Jesus." It may be taken either as the first two and the last letters of the word "Jesus" as spelled in Greek or as the first three. The forms shown in the illustration were stylized in a period when Greek was not understood by the clergy. Because they are so much in use, it is important to know correctly what they mean.

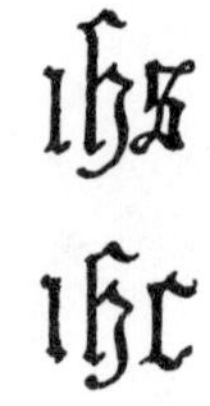

The Greek letters *X* (Chi) and *P* (Rho) are the first two letters of the word for Christ (*Xristos*) in the Greek language. They have been in use almost since the beginnings of Christian history.

The Greek letters Alpha and Omega shown in the illustration are the first and last letters of the Greek alphabet. In Christian usage they represent Christ as the beginning and end of all things. (See Rev. 22:13.)

Here we have a combination of the Chi-Rho and Alpha-Omega literary symbols, signifying Christ as the first and the last, coeternal with God the Father. These four letters properly belong together; Alpha and Omega standing by themselves are incomplete without the Chi-Rho or *IHS*.

This monogram represents *I*, the first letter of the word "Jesus" in Greek, and *X* (Chi) the first letter of the word "Christ" in Greek; the whole signifying Jesus Christ.

This partly literary symbol is commonly used but not commonly understood. It represents a fish, with the Greek word for fish inscribed upon it in capital letters.

[1] Symbols of the apostles and the passion of our Lord are omitted. For these and others less commonly chosen see my book *Christian Symbolism in the Evangelical Churches*. (New York and Nashville: Abingdon Press, 1942.)

From the letters of this Greek word an acrostic was made by the early Christians, the respective letters standing literally for "Jesus Christ, God's Son, Saviour." In times of persecution the Greek word for fish was used as a secret password by the Christians.

ΙΧΘΥC

These letters stand for *Iesus Nazarenus Rex Iudaeorum,* which is Latin for "Jesus of Nazareth, King of the Jews." This was the inscription placed on the cross of our Lord. (See John 19:19.)

INRI

The Latin type of cross, on which Christ was crucified, is the most important and characteristic symbol of the Christian faith. It is the cross most commonly used on an altar and has profound significance for believers, because it continually calls attention to the sacrifice of Christ for their salvation.

Tradition says that the apostle Andrew, at his own request, was crucified on a cross shaped like the Roman Letter *X*, because he deemed himself unworthy to be crucified on a cross similar to that on which Jesus died.

This is the Jerusalem or Crusader's Cross. It is said that it was discovered by Godfrey de Bouillon, a crusader who first governed the city of Jerusalem after it was captured from the Mohammedans. The four arms are said by some to signify the four Gospels. Sometimes four Greek crosses are inserted, one in each of the four quarters; these signifying that the gospel has been carried to the four corners of the earth. The original intention is not known. Its meaning is also connected with healing, because it is shaped like four crutches joined together.

The symmetrical Greek Cross has arms of equal length. This form of cross was in use among the Greeks for a long time prior to the coming of Christianity. It was to them a symbol of divine protection. It was early adopted by the Christians, and it is believed that as far back as the first century A.D. this form of cross was traced with water on the foreheads of infant children being baptized. In any case, signing thus with the cross is still practiced in the liturgical churches.

The Celtic Cross of Iona, Scotland, was an Irish invention. The circle represents eternity. The Irish missionary Columba (sixth century) introduced it into Scotland. Ancient Irish sculptors produced many beautiful examples of this type of cross. The Celtic Cross is much used today in chancels, church bulletins, books, tracts, and the like.

The cross and orb are symbolic of the truimph of the gospel of Christ throughout the whole world. This is one of the emblems borne by the ruler of England at coronation.

The Anchor Cross probably first came into use among the early Christians in the catacombs. Doubtless it has reference to Heb. 6:18, 19.

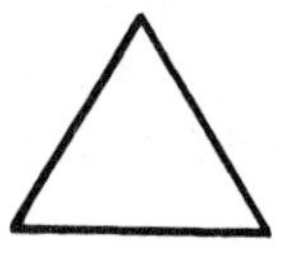

An equilateral triangle is a symbol of the Trinity—three distinct lines form one figure, signifying three Persons and one God. Sometimes an equilateral triangle is used with the word "Sanctus" on each member of the figure, meaning "Holy, Holy, Holy."

A circle appears to have no beginning and no end; therefore, it is used to represent eternity.

An equilateral triangle within a circle represents the timelessness of the divine Trinity.

A circle within an equilaterial triangle is a variant of the above form and has the same meaning.

Courtesy of Rider-Philpott Studio

National College for Christian Workers, Kansas City, Missouri

The triquetra was anciently used to represent the holy Trinity. Three equal arcs indicate eternity in continuous form, and the interweaving indicates indivisibility. At the center the combination forms an equilateral triangle which is another trinitarian symbol.

Three circles intertwined express the unity, equality, and eternity of the holy Trinity.

The fleur-de-lys is a beautiful trinitarian symbol of French origin. It is a stylized representation of the flower of the iris, which has three "standards" and three "falls."

A hand surrounded by a nimbus and rays, and reaching downward or upward, is a common symbol of God the Father and Creator. In Christian art the first Person of the Trinity is very rarely represented by a human form.

The dove is the principal symbol of the Holy Spirit. Doubtless the idea is derived from Mark 1:10, which refers to the descent of the Holy Spirit at the baptism of Jesus. There are other symbols which refer to the appearance of the Holy Spirit at Pentecost. They are not in common use in churches.

The lamb carrying the banner of victory represents Christ, triumphant over death and the grave, bearing the symbol of salvation.

Four winged creatures are used to symbolize the four evangelists who wrote the canonical Gospels:

A winged man represents Matthew, because his Gospel emphasizes Jesus' human descent.

Mark is represented by a lion, because of the phrase he used with reference to John the Baptist, "the voice of one crying in the wilderness," suggestive of a lion.

Luke is represented by an ox, an animal commonly used for sacrifice. The reference is to the full description of the crucifixion in Luke's gospel.

John soared to sublime heights in his revelation of the mind of Christ; and, therefore, an eagle is used to represent him as the most spiritual of the four evangelists.

The writers of the four Gospels are sometimes represented by their respective symbols on pulpits. A church named after any one of them may properly display the appropriate symbol at the main entrance to the church.

The five-pointed star is properly designated the Epiphany Star and has reference to the showing of the child Jesus to the wise men, representing the Gentiles. (See Num. 24:17; Matt. 2:1, 2.)

The Phoenix, a mythical bird which was said to burst into flames at its death and thereafter to rise immediately from its ashes, is a symbol of resurrection and immortality. This symbol is of Greek origin and is re-

lated to the burning of old palm trees and using the ashes to fertilize the seedlings. The Greek word for palm tree is *phoinix*.

A ship was used very early as a symbol of the Christian Church, because church buildings at first were often shaped somewhat like a ship of those times. This symbol is in common use today and is quite fitting in a chancel. It is sometimes used with reference to the missionary activities of the church.

The oil lamp is a common symbol of the Word of God. It is fitting for use on a pulpit.

The bursting pomegranate signifies the resurrection of Christ, who burst the tomb and came forth victorious over death to spread his influence throughout the world.

A butterfly is a beautiful symbol of resurrection. It breaks open the pupa and soars aloft into the sunlight with a new body, thus signifying the flight of the soul after death into a new and higher life.

Grapes usually signify the sacrament of Holy Communion. This symbol is in common use in chancels and often appears on Communion tables or altars.

Local innovations in the use of symbolism may sometimes lead to confusing results. For instance, an attempt to represent in stained glass each of the eight Beatitudes with an improvised symbol. However, the Beatitudes, because of their spiritual implications, do not lend themselves readily to representation by objective symbols. Perhaps it would be better to represent them with a scroll containing the word "Beatitudes" at the top and beneath it the Roman figures I to VIII inclusive, somewhat in the same manner as the Ten Commandments are usually represented.

— VII —

Stained Glass

STAINED GLASS IS SOMETIMES REFERRED TO AS "ART GLASS"; THE FORMER is the correct term.

If not too obtrusive, and if the quality of the glass and the workmanship are good, stained-glass windows in a chancel can do much to enhance its general appearance. This is especially true of churches built in either the Gothic or the Romanesque style.

On the other hand, a poorly designed window in such a prominent place in the church can be very annoying to the eye and distracting to the mind.

Stained-glass artists usually have difficulty in satisfactorily portraying the human face on a life-size scale, because the medium doesn't lend itself well for that purpose. Many stained-glass windows in churches are so overloaded with large wooden-looking human figures and artificial curlicues as to appear quite grotesque and bewildering to the average worshiper. Moreover, frequently, medieval-style lettering is used and the letters and words crowded together so as to be indecipherable a short distance away.

I have seen stained-glass church windows with Greek words and phrases and accompanying symbols that have no meaning for anybody except a scholar deeply versed in such matters. The effect is that of "speaking in an unknown tongue." This type of puzzle window may give pleasure to a learned clergyman but it inevitably bewilders the lay mind. Happily such stained-glass enigmas are becoming rare.

A good stained-glass window job is likely to be expensive. Therefore, it is important to secure the services of a skilled artist in this medium— one whose imagination can take hold of the idea for the design and work

Church of the Abiding Presence, Lutheran Theological Seminary, Gettysburg, Pennsylvania

it into a thing of beauty, keeping in mind always fitness and ecclesiastical good taste.

Generally, human figures should be kept relatively small in size and symbolism should predominate. The most effective colors are blues and reds in subdued tones.

The chief charm of stained glass is the kaleidoscopic shifting of tones and accents in the color as the light outside changes from cloud to sunshine and from dawn to dark throughout the day. This almost magical effect is lacking in stained-glass chancel windows which are completely shut off from outside light and which have to be artificially illuminated from the back.

Some authorities say that a stained-glass window in the chancel, above the altar, tends to spoil its total effect and interferes with the unity of worship. This is most likely to be so if strong sunlight falls directly on the chancel windows during the morning service. In such a situation it is well to have the colors in the stained glass toned down enough to avoid a glaring effect. Of course, a circular rose window may be placed high enough above the altar to avoid such an effect. In case it is decided to have the usual type of large stained-glass windows in the chancel, on account of their dominant position they should be carefully designed with a central major motif. For this purpose a representation of Christ is commonly chosen.

The process of making a stained-glass window is quite intricate and calls for highly developed artistic and technical skills. Working drawings of the design are made to full size. From these a tracing is made to show the lead lines by which the cutter is guided in cutting the glass. The various pieces of glass must be carefully selected with reference to color effect and complement or contrast to the adjoining pieces. All the pieces are fixed in proper position on a sheet of plate glass with hot wax, and the whole is then covered with pigment. While wet, the coating is stippled to let light through; and when it is dry, various tools are used to pick out lights and half tones. The patterns are worked out either by painting them on in thick opaque lines or by etching the paint out according to the design. Staining consists in painting the back with nitrate of silver and heating it so as to obtain various colors ranging from pale yellow to deep orange. Then the various pieces of glass are dismounted, placed on iron trays, and brought to a white heat in a kiln.

Heating incorporates the pigmentation in the glass while it is in a molten state, and thereafter the color is irremovable except by use of hydrofluoric acid. The glazier then puts the stained-glass pieces together according to the artist's design and joins them with grooved leads and solder.

From the foregoing sketch it will be evident that good work of this type commands a relatively high price. As a rule, cost will be closely related to the area to be covered and the amount of detail required.

— VIII —

Flags

NOWADAYS IN AMERICA ONE FREQUENTLY SEES TWO FLAGS DISPLAYED in Christian churches, one symbolizing the Christian religion, the other being the national flag.

The flag now commonly called "the Christian flag," although it has not been officially adopted by any Christian denomination, has generally taken the place of one formerly used in Protestant churches, which bore a cross and the Latin inscription *In hoc signo vinces*, reminiscent of the victory of Emperor Constantine over Maxentius, A.D. 312. Of course, as used on the above-mentioned church flag, the motto was intended to suggest the conquest of the world for Christ. Gradually this flag came to be regarded as not well suited for world-wide use, especially in missionary fields, because it seemed to bear a connotation of imperialism.

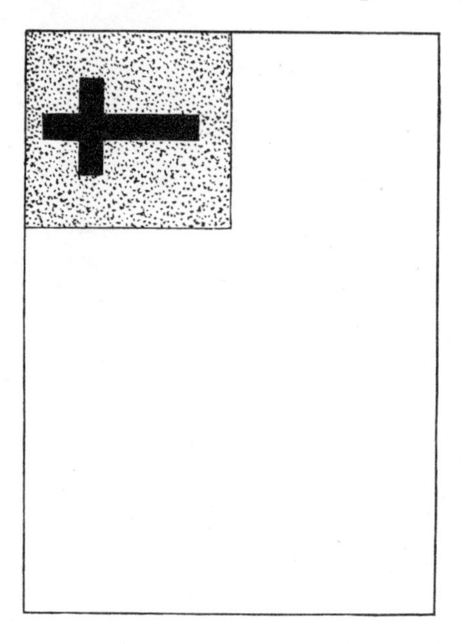

THE CHRISTIAN FLAG

The design of the present-day Christian flag originated with a Sunday-school superintendent, Charles C. Overton, at Brighton Chapel, Staten Island, New York. On Rally Day, September 26, 1897, a special speaker was expected to make an address at the chapel. He missed his appointment and Mr. Overton filled in the time with an extemporaneous talk on the symbolic value of flags. Pointing to the United States' flag draped on the piano, he suggested that Sunday schools and churches should have a distinctive flag. He remarked that it should be white to signify purity and peace, and in the upper left-hand corner it should contain a red cross on a blue field —the cross to represent Christ's sacrificial death for all mankind; the blue ground to signify faith, trust, sincerity; the whole to be symbolic of peace on earth, good will among men.

This spontaneous idea of a design for a Christian flag lay more or less fallow in Overton's mind for a decade, until the year 1907, when it was brought by him to the attention of Ralph E. Diffendorfer, who was at that time secretary of the Methodist Young People's Missionary Movement. The idea made a strong appeal to Dr. Diffendorfer; and he, with Overton, consulted a leading flagmaker in New York City, who consented to make the flag on order.

Dr. Diffendorfer took the new flag to summer conferences of his organization and helped to popularize it. The following year at a leadership conference he spoke of the new flag and expressed the desire that a pledge, similar to the salute to the national flag, might be written for it. At the close of the meeting Lynn Harold Hough, at that time the pastor of the church, presented to Dr. Diffendorfer the words of the now familiar salute to the Christian flag: "I pledge allegiance to my flag and the Saviour for whose kingdom it stands; one brotherhood uniting all mankind in service and love."

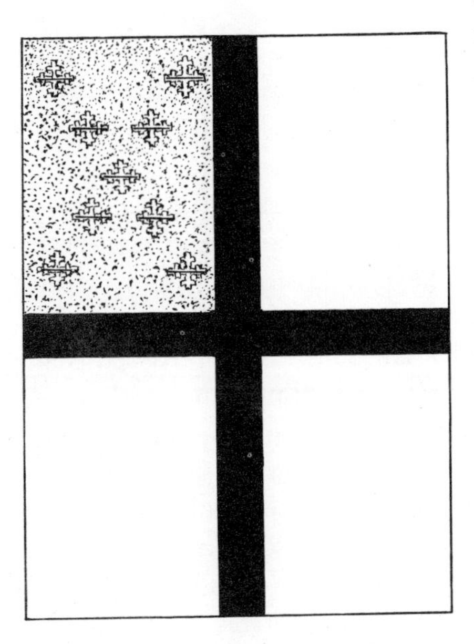

THE EPISCOPAL FLAG

Subsequently, Dr. Hough substituted the words "the Christian" for "my." [1]

On October 16, 1940, the Protestant Episcopal Church adopted a beautiful flag which is rapidly coming into use in Episcopal churches. A devoted Episcopal layman named

[1] The story of the Christian flag was told to me by the late Ralph E. Diffendorfer, and confirmed by Lynn Harold Hough, especially with reference to the salute.

William M. Baldwin, of Long Island, New York, was the father of the idea which he had turned over in his mind for nearly twenty years. The flag was finally designed by Pierre La Rose, a leading American authority on heraldry, who contributed his services free.

The symbolism of this flag is interesting. The white field stands for purity, the red cross on the white field represents the blood of the martyrs. The blue of the dexter chief in the upper left-hand corner is the light sky-blue color known as "Madonna blue." The nine white cross-crosslets on the blue field represent the nine original dioceses of the Protestant Episcopal Church. They are symbolic of the spread of Christianity and are arranged in the form of a Saint Andrew's Cross to commemorate the fact that after the Revolutionary War, Bishop Seabury (the first American Episcopal bishop) was ordained by the non-juring bishops of the Church of Scotland—the archbishops of York and Canterbury being at that time uncertain of their constitutional authority to ordain a bishop from a land no longer in British possession.

The flag of the Roman Catholic Church has the papal arms for its emblem.

The United States' government prescribes rules for the display of the national flag in armed service usage; but there is no binding federal law regarding civilian usage, although some individual states have enacted such laws.

The Christian flag used by the U.S. Navy is a triangular pennant of white with a blue Latin cross at the center. It is flown above the U.S. national flag during divine worship. The U.S. Army flag for chaplains is a blue rectangle with a white Latin cross.

In June, 1942, a joint Congressional resolution was adopted codifying "existing rules and customs pertaining to the display and use of the U.S. flag in public places." This resolution is hortatory but not binding. It is quite similar to the rules previously compiled in Washington, D.C., by sixty-eight patriotic societies. According to these rules, when the United States flag is carried in procession, it should have the place of honor, which is on the right hand of the column, any other flag being on the left. If there is a line of flags, the United States flag should be carried alone in front of the center of the line.

If the church flag and the American flag are flown from a halyard, the American flag should be at the peak. No other flag should be flown

Courtesy of Hedrich-Blessing

First Baptist Church, Kalamazoo, Michigan

above the American flag. If the flags fly from adjacent staffs, the American flag is raised first and lowered last.

This is a secular code, essentially military in significance. Nowadays inside a church one usually finds the Christian, or church flag, on the right of the congregation as it looks forward. This special church usage is based on the assumption that inside the church the flag bearing the cross as a symbol of Christianity takes precedence over any national emblem.

The following is the substance of a resolution on display of flags in church passed by the Federal (now National) Council of the Churches of Christ in the U.S.A., January 23, 1942:

WHEREAS, The Federal Council of the Churches of Christ in the United States of America has received overtures and inquiries concerning the appropriate use and position of flags within the sanctuary dedicated to the worship of God; therefore be it

Resolved, That the Executive Committee, . . . without attempting to prescribe regulations, offers the following observations as advice to the churches:

(1) The Cross itself is generally accepted as a good and sufficient symbol for the house of God in the Christian tradition, without the use of a church flag.

(2) If the flag or banner representing the loyalty of the church to its Head is used along with the flag of the nation in the sanctuary, the symbol of loyalty to God should have the place of highest honor.

(3) According to tradition, ancient and modern, the place of highest honor is to the right, on the floor level of the congregation; in the chancel or on any level above that of the floor of the congregation, to the right of the clergyman as he faces the congregation.

(4) The form most generally regarded as the Christian flag for display in churches is a white rectangle with a blue rectangular field in the upper corner (at the mast side) containing a red Latin cross. This flag is recognized, however, only by general usage and not by official action of any ecclesiastical body.

Whether one follows the military code or the resolution on this subject which was adopted by the Federal Council of the Churches of Christ is a matter of choice. At present there is a lack of uniformity in practice.

If heated local argument about the relative positions of the national flag and the Christian flag is likely to develop, it may be wise to have no flag at all. A somewhat awkward compromise may be effected by placing the national flag outside the chancel at the right of the congregation as it looks forward, and by placing the Christian flag at the right of the minister inside the chancel. This arrangement gives a place of honor to both flags and may quiet criticism.

The cross in a church is a sufficient symbol of the Christian religion, without a flag of any kind. In any case it is better to have no flag at all than to have a church quarrel over such a minor matter. Presumably we may soon have more or less discussion about the place, if any, of the flag of the United Nations in a church.

The idea of placing flags in churches is primarily military in origin and was derived from Europe.

Flags are not an essential requirement in church equipment. My personal preference is the exclusion of all flags from the chancel.

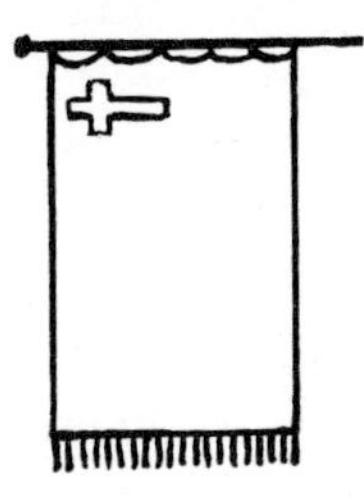

— IX —

Flowers

MANY CHURCHGOERS SEEM TO BE OF THE OPINION THAT THE MORE flowers that can be crowded, on almost any occasion, into the chancel space the better. However, flowers are somewhat like candles; where there are too many, and especially if they are badly arranged, the effect may be quite disturbing to the eye.

If many flowers are brought to church in summertime when they are plentiful in home gardens, they ought to be tastefully arranged in a few large containers rather than spread all over the chancel in small lots that make the place look as if a flower show were in progress.

Flowers for the vases on the altar should seldom be in more than one or two colors. They should *never* be artificial. Generally, white flowers are to be preferred, as they are always in good taste and harmonize readily with seasonal colored vestments used on pulpit and lectern.

THE CROSS OBSCURED

On account of dampness be sure to keep potted plants away from any surface that is in danger of being soiled or permanently marked, or see that mats or plates are put under them to hold the moisture.

Do not place flowers in positions where they are likely to be knocked down by movements of choir members or of the minister. No matter how large the pulpit may be, do not place flowers on it; the same rule applies to the baptismal font.

If flowers are placed in vases on an altar or Communion table, they should not be put behind a cross, because they may have the effect of obscuring it. In the chancel flowers should never be permitted to stand so as to obscure a cross, a significant carving, or a picture.

Perhaps an altar would look more effective if flowers were placed in vases on low tables at the right and left of it, in order that the top of the altar might be kept free of everything except the cross and the candles. Of course, when Holy Communion is being administered, the principal equipment regarded as essential for that sacrament is properly in place on the altar; and there is little or no space to spare for flowers.

If flowers are placed on the altar, they should have the effect of leading up to the cross and thus bring out and adorn its significance. *It is better to err in the direction of simplicity than to overload.* Restraint makes for dignity. Overdecoration is an indication of bad taste and bad judgment. Two vases of flowers may be quite pleasing; four vases may look commonplace or gaudy.

Regarding vases, it may be said that those one sees in churches are frequently much too large and, therefore, are expensive to fill. Besides, when they are filled, they are apt to look showy—an effect which is not to be desired in church. When purchasing vases for church use, select those with a wide mouth; because this permits better arrangement of the flowers. It would be well to have vases weighted at the bottom in order to increase their stability. Sand serves well enough for this purpose. Always keep empty vases off the altar.

Flowers should be put in place and arranged, by a member, or members, of the altar guild, a half hour or more before the service of worship begins.

Flowers placed in the altar vases should be closely similar in color and graceful in arrangement. By all means avoid the appearance of stiffness. Generally speaking, flowers should not rise much more than one and one-half times the height of the vase or container in which they are placed. Wiring may be necessary for certain kinds of flowers, the stems of which tend easily to droop.

After the worship services are over, it is customary in a good many churches to send the flowers used in the chancel to sick persons and shut-ins. It is not customary to return them to the homes of those who gave them.

If the church provides for changing paraments (hangings used in the sanctuary) and altar antependia in keeping with the seasons of the Christian Year, it would be well for the altar guild to see that, as far as possible, the color of the flowers used on or near the altar corresponds fairly closely with the liturgical color of the day or season. White is an appropriate color of flowers used for weddings, also for funerals. White is the color for Easter Sunday. White flowers look well with almost any kind of background. Red flowers are used for Christmas and Pentecost Sunday. All Palm Sunday decorations should be taken away after the services of that day. Flowers should not be on display anywhere in the church during Holy Week, which is penitential in its significance.

A properly arranged altar will look impressive enough without flowers, in case none are available on any particular Sunday. In fact, at times, occasional lack of flowers on the altar may have a good effect.

If a harvest festival is held in the church annually, flowers, sheaves of grain, foliage of trees, fruits, and the like may be abundantly used in the chancel; but packaged or canned goods should ordinarily be excluded, because a grocery-store effect seems undesirable in church. At least there is no excuse for using canned goods in a church which has ready access to farms.

Most of the church-supply houses can furnish attractive altar flower charts on which can be entered by the altar guild the names of those who are willing to donate flowers on certain Sundays. The donors may wish to have mentioned in the church bulletin the deceased person, or persons, for whom the flowers are given as a memorial. A flower chart is generally displayed in the vestibule or narthex.

Some churches establish a small endowment fund in memory of a deceased member of the congregation who was greatly respected and beloved. The income is used to buy flowers regularly or for Sundays with no listed donors. When such a fund is available, perhaps the altar guild can secure the best service by dealing with one reliable florist who understands the tastes and needs of those concerned. At times it may be advisable to invite the florist's assistance in choosing flowers whose color will have a good effect when seen from the line of pews farthest from the chancel.

Certain kinds of flowers are best if selected in the bud stage; so that they may be properly open, but not ready to disintegrate, when exposed in church, where the atmosphere is much warmer than in a florist's refrigerator.

It is best to water flowers with fresh water at room temperature.

Courtesy of Haskell

Quincy Point Congregational Church, Quincy, Massachusetts

Those with succulent stems should be split at the bottom of the stem for a half inch or more. This practice is said to promote the absorption of water. Some flower lovers believe that a tablet of aspirin or two put in the water in which flowers stand will improve their condition and make them last longer. In any case the aspirin will do no harm. Others use a small portion of one of the plant stimulants found in various stores.

Among the favorite flowers that stand up well in church decoration are lilies, dahlias, carnations, and gladioli—particularly the last mentioned. Gladioli are free of odor and, therefore, do not offend sensitive or allergic nostrils. For the same reason they are excellent flowers to send to sick persons, after the worship service is over. In recent decades gladioli have been developed to an amazing degree of beauty. Carnations have a pleasant odor and keep well. They are also very desirable for use in the chancel.

Japanese primroses should be avoided. They are very poisonous to some people, and it is said that not all men who work in greenhouses can approach them with impunity. Potted azaleas and cyclamens are as beautiful as potted Japanese primroses and have the great merit of being safe to handle.

The odor of a great bank of Easter lilies is quite heavy and cannot be endured for long by persons who are bothered by the perfume.

In the choice of flowers for use in the church the altar guild must be governed by considerations of color, beauty, symmetry of stems and leaves, and freedom from ill effects upon sensitive persons. In regard to color special thought must be given to the carrying effect when seen from a distance equal to the length of the nave of the church. Also, churchly restraint must be constantly kept in mind. It is well to avoid setting up flowers in the shape of stars, crosses, triangles, or any other sacred symbolic form. Let them speak entirely through the symbolism of color and their natural beauty.

Flowers are commonly used in profusion at weddings. At funerals, especially at funerals of well-known persons, the attempt to crowd all the flowers into and near the chancel sometimes produces an ostentatious effect which is undesirable. Increasingly, bereaved relatives are asking that flowers not be sent to funerals; but if the friends are so disposed, they are asked to make a donation to a charity or cause which was favored by the deceased during his or her lifetime, or to the flower fund of the parish.

FLOWERS

Extravagant display of one kind or another at funerals is an American custom which has been cultivated painstakingly by morticians and florists for altogether too long. It is high time for a change toward more simplicity and greater economy. In many cases far too much of the meager insurance money available after death for a man's widow and family is expended on a brief, costly, and quickly perishable display.

— X —

Vestments

IN MOST EVANGELICAL CHURCHES TODAY, IDEAS ABOUT VESTMENTS ARE more or less in a state of confusion—a condition which may be traced back to the origins of Protestantism in the Reformation. At that time the reformers were inclined to associate elaborate robes, such as the chasuble, with the exercise of sacerdotal powers. Apparently they were quite uncertain as to the proper garb to be used for the conduct of divine worship. Sometimes the officiant would appear in his doctor's robe or in a simple university gown or perhaps in a monk's habit. And again, the very same officiant would appear in the historic priestly vestments used for many centuries by the Roman Catholic clergy. This lack of rule or order in regard to vestments has prevailed among Protestant ministers until the present day.

Even in the Protestant Episcopal and the various Lutheran churches which are avowedly liturgical, there is no uniform rule regarding the garb to be worn by a minister during divine worship. Some Anglo-Catholic priests celebrating "Mass" are scarcely distinguishable from Roman Catholic priests. Generally, the low-church Episcopal priests are vested simply in cassock, surplice, and stole—plain vestments that some day may be generally recognized as quite proper for clergymen in the free churches. They were well established prior to the Middle Ages, when ornamentation and elaborateness became common.

The extreme ministerial reactionaries in the Reformation movement, because of their desire to get rid of everything suggestive of Romanism, wore no clerical robes at all; and this feeling was transmitted to America by many of the Puritan colonists. The black robe which was then much in use in the Anglican Church was commonly used by the American Episcopal clergy two hundred years ago, as well as by some of the first

Courtesy of John Russell Pope, architect—Eggers and Higgins, successors

First Congregational Church, Columbus, Ohio

Lutheran clergymen who came to America. The present-day vestment usage of Episcopal and of a good many Lutheran clergymen is much more nearly in accord with historic pre-Reformation usage. It is now clearly seen that there is nothing distinctively Protestant or clerical about the black robe, and, moreover, that the simple vestments worn by ministers in the early Christian Church are not a badge of either sacerdotalism or priestly separation from the people.

Today, wherever any robe at all is used in the free churches, it is likely to be the black robe. At least it can be said that its use makes for decorum, and it has the minor merit of covering up any eccentricity of dress to which the minister may be prone. It tends to promote a feeling of respect for the office of the ministry. It is more distinctively appropriate wear for a clergyman, officiating in church, than the Prince Albert coat which, years ago, was also the garb of speechmaking politicians, or than the cutaway coat and striped trousers so commonly worn by morticians today.

Unfortunately the black robe can hardly be dissociated from its university background. It is reminiscent of college commencements, the more so if the minister wishes to display university distinctions by chevrons, facings, and hoods. These are not desirable for church services, except perhaps on certain occasions, such as when a baccalaureate sermon is being preached.

The use of the black robe by clergymen is rapidly increasing in Protestant churches throughout this country, and perhaps one should be thankful that it is. Wonder of wonders, for a good many years now we have had robed or surpliced choirs; but, until recently, most Protestants have been very squeamish about seeing the minister, as the leader of worship, garbed with due regard for his ministerial office. Indeed, we are still so squeamish that any minister in the so-called nonliturgical churches who would make bold to appear in his pulpit in any ecclesiastical vestment other than the black robe is likely to be spoken of as a "high churchman."

Of course in the free churches the clothing worn by ministers is a matter of personal choice.

Clerical collars, rabatos (stiff flaring collars), and neck bands are not ecclesiastical vestments in the strict sense.

The three basic churchly and historic vestments of the clergy are the cassock, surplice, and stole. There are others, but the aforementioned three constitute the simplest dress of a minister in a liturgical church. For information they may be briefly described as follows:

1. The cassock is a lightweight, long garment made of black serge or silk, closely form fitting from neck to waist, flowing from waist to

CASSOCK, SURPLUS, AND STOLE

ankles. The sleeves are narrow. In Catholic usage it is closely buttoned down the front; in Anglican usage on the side; in Lutheran usage it is a matter of choice, if such a garment is used by the minister at all. In the Episcopal churches the cassock of a bishop is violet and that of a Doctor of Divinity, scarlet.

2. A surplice is worn over a cassock and is made of fine white linen of good quality. It has full sleeves which are usually pointed. It reaches to a position slightly below the knees. It should not be ornamented.

3. A stole is a long, narrow band of variable width made of silk or brocade. It is draped over the shoulders, the narrowest part at the back of the neck. From the shoulders downward it increases in width and is finished with a fringe. It usually bears a cross or *IHS* monogram a short distance above the fringe. Stoles are made in colors to suit the day or season of the Christian Year.

Cassock, surplice or abbreviated surplice (cotta), and stole are often worn by choristers in nonliturgical churches. However, the stole is said to be symbolic of a minister's devotion to his labors in obedience to Christ. Indeed, it is said to symbolize "the yoke of Christ" which the minister assumes at ordination, when the stole is first placed upon his shoulders.

Hesitancy in the matter of adopting such ecclesiastical vestments is partly grounded in Protestant fear of what the few brethren who always want to go too far may do. So long as there is no church law to restrain such persons in such matters, extremists will be in evidence here and there.

Overelaboration of vestments and church equipment is foreign to distinctively Protestant tradition, usage, and outlook. Candor compels one to say that fear of the formalism they might lead to is not to be lightly regarded.

— XI —

Seasons and Colors

THE NATIONAL COUNCIL OF CHURCHES RECOMMENDS AN ADAPTED FORM of the traditional Christian Year, prepared mainly with a view to meeting the needs, preferences, and restraints of the free churches. In this plan provision is made for seven seasons, in the following order: Advent; Christmastide; Epiphanytide; Lent; Eastertide; Whitsuntide (Pentecost); Kingdomtide (corresponding in good part to the Trinity season observed by Lutherans and Episcopalians).

The cycle of seasons in this rearrangement of the Christian Year is indicated and explained as follows:

ADVENT—Begins on the fourth Sunday preceding Christmas. It contains four Sundays.

CHRISTMASTIDE—Extends from Christmas Day to Twelfth Night (January 5).

EPIPHANYTIDE—Extends from January 6 to the day before Ash Wednesday. It contains four to nine Sundays, depending on the date of Easter.

LENT—Begins with Ash Wednesday and ends with Saturday of Holy Week. It includes the forty weekdays and six Sundays preceding Easter. It includes Passion Sunday (the second Sunday before Easter) and Palm Sunday (one week before Easter Sunday).

EASTERTIDE—Begins with Easter Sunday and lasts forty-nine days. It includes seven Sundays.

WHITSUNTIDE—Whitsunday, or Pentecost, comes fifty days after Easter and celebrates the descent of the Holy Spirit. Whitsuntide may contain from eleven to fifteen Sundays.

KINGDOMTIDE—Begins with the Festival of Christ the King, on the last Sunday in August (one of the innovations in the new calendar), and ends with the fourth Saturday preceding Christmas. Because of its great length, it covers a period in which a good many of the generally recognized special days occur. There are Labor Sunday, Rally Day in the church school,

World Communion Sunday, Reformation Sunday, All Saints Day, World Peace Sunday, and Thanksgiving Day.

Many of these special days lend themselves to preaching on various phases of the social gospel or Christianity in action—themes which are especially appropriate in Kingdomtide.

The fact that Easter is a movable feast constantly disturbs the setup of the Christian Year. Because Easter is determined by the Sunday following the full moon which appears on, or next after, the spring equinox, Easter may occur on March 22 or any following date through April 25—a range of thirty-five days.

As the date of Easter affects the major part of the Christian Year, it is interesting to review briefly the bitter controversy that preceded the determination of the date as it is now observed in the Western churches of Christendom.

There is no mention of any special church festivals in the New Testament. However, it is evident that, quite early in the life of the Christian Church, some ancient usages in regard to Jewish festivals were influential in causing the institution of corresponding Christian Festivals. Many scholars believe that Easter derives from the Jewish Passover. Probably the Jerusalem church, or Jewish Christians of the Dispersion, set the pattern in this regard. The use of the word paschal in many languages in connection with Easter is confirmatory of this. Scholars say that the word paschal is derived from both Hebrew and Aramaic, in both of which it refers to the Passover festival.

Quite early in the history of Christianity there are records of very sharp disagreement between the Jewish and Gentile Christians regarding the date of the Easter observance. It is said that this debate was a principal reason for the Council of Nicea (A.D. 325), which was called by Emperor Constantine. The Jewish Christians wanted Easter to correspond with the celebration of the Passover, irrespective of the day of the week. The Gentile Christians, quite naturally, wanted to celebrate it on a Sunday. The Council of Nicea directed that the celebration of Easter should always be on a Sunday, the date to be calculated by astronomers at Alexandria; Easter Day to be on the first Sunday after the full moon immediately following the spring equinox. Very soon afterward, a difficulty arose from the fact that the appearance of the Easter

Courtesy of Macy

First Christian Church, Clinton, Illinois

moon varies in different longitudes, and there were other difficulties involving the erroneous Julian calendar in use at that time.

The correction of the calendar by Gregory XIII, in 1582, in close conformity with astronomical observation, and the consequent rectification of the date of Easter is now generally accepted in all the Western Christian churches, although the change was not made in Great Britain until 1752. The Eastern Orthodox churches, owing to dislike of anything issuing from Rome, did not accept the Gregorian correction of the calendar; so that the celebration of the Easter festival in those churches very rarely coincides with the date observed in the Western churches.

Many Protestant churches are now using with good effect paraments of various colors in keeping with the mood of the season of the Church Year. This practice belongs with observance of the Christian Year, either in the traditional or the new order, and has no necessary high-church implications. Obviously, the God we worship takes delight in marvelous seasonal changes of colors outdoors.

A brief survey of the usual interpretation of liturgical colors follows:

WHITE—Signifies purity, innocence. It is generally used on special days with reference to Jesus and the Trinity, also at baptism, confirmation, marriage, and ordination.

VIOLET or PURPLE—Signifies penitence, passion, suffering. They are used for Advent and Lent.

BLACK—Signifies mourning and death, and is used on Good Friday and at funerals.

RED—Signifies fire and blood. It is used for honoring the Holy Spirit and Christian martyrs.

GREEN—Signifies life, growth, hope, and immortality. It is properly used throughout the Kingdomtide season. However, the Festival of Christ the King, which begins this season, is marked by white.

The application of the above-mentioned colors to the seasons and special days of the Christian Year, as outlined previously, is as follows:

During the four Sundays of Advent, the first being the Sunday nearest November 30, violet is used. White is used during Christmastide and on Epiphany Day. Green is used during the remainder of the Epiphany season. Purple or violet is used through Lent, except black is used on Good Friday, as indicated above. However, this plan may be varied by using white during the first four weeks of Lent, red during the fifth week, and black during the last week. Easter Sunday calls for white, and this color is used until Whitsunday, or Pentecost, for which the proper color is red. For Trinity Sunday (the first Sunday after Pentecost) white is used. The remainder of the Sundays in Whitsuntide call for green. The Festival of Christ the King calls for white; the remainder of the Kingdomtide season calls for use of green.

The foregoing correlation of seasons, days, and colors is aligned as closely as possible with the traditional use of liturgical colors; but as there are no binding regulations regarding such use to be observed in the free churches, the variation suggested with reference to the Lenten season may be adopted in any church, if it so desires.

— XII —

Altar Guild

TODAY A GOOD MANY PROTESTANT CHURCHES HAVE A SPECIAL COMmittee in charge of matters concerned with preparation of the elements for the administration of the Lord's Supper; the changing of seasonal paraments and altar vestments, if any; placement of flowers in the chancel; disposal of flowers after use; and other similar duties. If there is a chancel of the commonest type, with a center pulpit, Communion table, and rail, the committee in charge of such matters may be fittingly called a "chancel committee." If the church has an altar and a divided chancel, the organization in charge of the chancel may be called an "altar guild." However, it is a matter of choice. Most of the suggestions given in this chapter are applicable to either situation.

As has been noted previously, a Communion table with a cross and candlesticks on it, is really a form of altar. Therefore, there is nothing particularly high church about using the name altar guild for the committee that looks after matters concerning the appearance of the chancel, whether it is divided or undivided. In the remainder of this chapter "altar guild" is used accordingly.

When reference is made to the chancel in this chapter, it means the space enclosed within and behind the Communion rail, or whatever it is that divides the space where the minister and his lay assistants conduct the entire service of worship from the space occupied by the congregation.

If the altar guild is properly organized and trained to care for the space enclosed in the chancel, it will add considerably to the smoothness with which chancel functions proceed, either during the Sunday services or on weekdays when there is a special service. Neglect of this duty or slipshod preparation may cause embarrassment at times, especially with regard to the administration of sacraments.

First Evangelical United Brethren Church, Hammond, Indiana

The work of the altar guild affords an opportunity for devout women of the church to render an important and interesting supplementary ministry. Its membership should be carefully chosen; and a president, vice-president, and secretary-treasurer should be elected annually. It is well to arrange for a monthly meeting at which duties can be assigned and matters of particular interest concerning the sanctuary discussed. Meetings should be opened with prayer, and occasionally a paper on some subject in connection with the ornaments and equipment of the chancel should be read by a member who has made a special study of it.

If a special room can be provided for the use of the committee, essential equipment, such as candles and linens, can be properly classified and stored in drawers provided for the purpose. If the church regularly observes the mood of each season of the Christian Year by use of various colored paraments for pulpit and lectern, and antependia for the altar, proper arrangements should be made for storage and care. When necessary, altar vestments should be changed not less than half an hour before the Sunday-morning worship service begins. Perhaps the major part of preparation for the administration of Holy Communion at a Sunday-morning service had best be done not later than the Saturday evening before. At latest, everything should be in order an hour before the Communion service begins.

Brass ornaments, vessels, and so forth on the altar or on a Communion table should always be handled with a fine cloth or chamois skin and not touched directly by hand.

Stubs of good-quality altar candles can be saved and may be returnable for allowance to the dealer from whom they were purchased. This is especially true of high-grade beeswax candles.

Altar candles should be placed so as to avoid danger of fire, especially if the altar is in a drafty location. The Church Fire Insurance Corporation of New York reports paying losses on eighty-eight fires in churches due to altar candles, in a period of twenty-three years of experience. Evidently the fire hazard from altar lights is not great, yet it is worth thinking about.

Reference should be made to the chapter entitled, "Flowers," for information about the display and handling of flowers within the chancel space. Flowers should not be allowed to stand more than a day without renewal of the water in the vases. When they are removed, the water should be poured out and the vases thoroughly rinsed with fresh water.

After the Sunday services it is a general custom to distribute the flowers used in the chancel to sick persons and shut-ins.

It is possible to obtain from church-supply houses beautiful charts on which may be entered the names of persons who agree to supply flowers for chancel use on certain Sundays. The chart can be displayed in the narthex, or vestibule, near the principal doorway of the church.

If a Bible, instead of a cross, is displayed on the altar, it should be opened before a worship service and closed shortly afterward. Otherwise, if the Bible is left constantly open, dust is likely to accumulate on it during the cleaning of the church or when there is much fine dust in suspension in the air. This precaution is especially necessary in large cities where there is much air pollution. The Bible itself is an important symbol in a Protestant church; and, in any case, it should be treated with respect and care. In some city churches flags are covered between services. This tends to make the cloth last longer.

While members of the altar guild are at work in the chancel, it is proper to move about quietly and talk in a low voice. The chancel contains the holy of holies of the church; the worship center; in fact, the sanctuary proper. Therefore, it is a place associated with sacred functions; and it should be treated with reverential respect at all times. Unfortunately a great many Protestants have not been taught this lesson.

The members of the altar guild can do much to educate the other members of the church to have due respect for its sacred precincts and appurtenances. Some of this instruction might well be imparted in the kindergarten of the church school.

In most Protestant churches today, individual Communion cups are used in trays for convenience in serving and also for hygienic reasons. The problem of disposing of the unused elements after the Communion service is over must be settled. In some denominations the rubric directs that such remains be consumed by the minister and his assistants. Perhaps a better rule is to pour out the unused consecrated grape juice on mother earth. To pour it back into a container for future reconsecration and use is not to be commended. Having been exposed and perhaps slightly contaminated, it should either be consumed immediately or poured out as recommended above. Unless this duty is reserved for himself by the pastor, it may be assigned to some member of the altar guild.

In a great many churches the unused wafers, or pieces of unleavened bread, are stored for future use. Consecrated bread should not be thrown in a garbage can under any circumstances.

Linens used at the service of Holy Communion should be carefully laundered after each use. Linens for use in the chancel should be of the highest grade obtainable; they will last longer and look better than those of poor quality.

Water should be provided by the altar guild in advance of a baptismal service which is to be held during or after the worship service. If there is a baptismal font, it should be filled with fresh water before a baptism. If there is no font, a bowl will serve quite as well; and it should be held by an attendant or placed on a convenient table near the minister. It is well also to have a small hand towel near by, which the minister can use to remove the moisture from his fingers before picking up the ritual to complete the baptismal service. This detail can be left in care of a member of the altar guild.

Glossary

ADMINISTRATION—The application of a rite or sacrament, such as baptism, confirmation, or the Lord's Supper, to a person or persons individually.

ALTAR—From the Latin *ara*, meaning altar. The Communion table, "the Lord's Table," where the elements are consecrated.

ALTAR FALL—A name occasionally applied to an altar vestment.

ALTAR GUILD—The committee of women organized for care of the altar of a church. Sometimes called the "*chancel committee.*"

ANTEPENDIUM—From the Latin *ante*, before; and *pendere*, to hang. A parament suspended from the altar, pulpit, or lectern.

AUDITORIUM—A term often used for the portion of the church where the congregation sits.

BANDS—White linen appendages affixed to the collars of clergymen in certain churches. In the past, bands were also worn by judges and lawyers. They are not ecclesiastical vestments.

BAPTISTERY—The place in a church where baptism is administered. In churches which regularly practice baptism by immersion it is essentially a tank in an enclosed space.

BRANCH LIGHTS—Candles in holders mounted on an arm set upon a single base (a candelabrum). The arm may support from three to seven lights.

CANDLE LIGHTER—A tubular instrument into which a lighting taper may be inserted. It has a bell-shaped device for extinguishing lighted candles.

CASSOCK—A black garment over which a surplice, stole, or other vestment may be worn.

CELEBRATION—Performance of a sacred ceremony or rite. In distinctively liturgical churches the one who performs the rite is sometimes called a "celebrant."

CHANCEL—From the Latin *cancelli*, screen latticework. The part of the church building containing the altar and choir, sometimes separated from the nave by a railing or screen. It is generally a few steps higher than the nave. *See* SANCTUARY.

CLERGYMAN—From the Greek *kleros*, lot inheritance. Hence, an allotted office.

COTTA—From the Italian *cotta*, coat. A short surplice, usually worn by choristers.

DOSSAL OR DORSAL—The cloth hung permanently back of and above the altar, if there is no reredos.

ELEMENTS—The bread and wine used in the celebration of the Lord's Supper. In the distinctively liturgical churches a third element, water, is used to dilute the wine, because it is believed that blood and water flowed from the spear wound in the Saviour's side during the crucifixion. In preference to alcoholic wine most Protestant churches use unfermented grape juice, which contains a preservative.

EUCHARIST—From the Greek *eucharistia*, thanksgiving. The sacrament of Holy Communion, which primarily involves thanksgiving for the oblation and sacrifice of Jesus Christ. Somehow in Protestant thinking, this simple ecclesiastical term has been given a sacerdotal connotation.

EUCHARISTIC LIGHTS—The two large candles placed one on either side of the altar cross, or of the altar itself, during celebration of the Lord's Supper. They represent Christ's two natures—human and divine. All other altar lights are secondary in significance.

FAIR LINEN—The topmost, linen, altar cloth.

FONT—From the Latin *fons*, fountain. A container for the water used in baptism.

FRONTAL—A hanging cloth which covers the front of the altar completely.

FRONTLET—*See* SUPERFRONTAL.

GRADIN—From the Latin *gradus*, step. A step or shelf (behind the altar) which is higher than the mensa. This shelf usually bears the cross and candlesticks. Sometimes at the middle of the gradin there is a somewhat higher, narrow step, on which the cross is placed. In the distinctively liturgical churches this narrow step is called a "throne."

HOLY COMMUNION—The Lord's Supper.

LAYING ON OF HANDS—Placing the hands of the officiant on the head of a person being baptized, confirmed, or ordained. A very ancient Christian practice mentioned in the New Testament.

LECTERN—(Sometimes spelled LECTURN when it refers to the kind of desk that swings around on a pivot.) From the Latin *legere*, to read. The reading desk from which the minister reads passages from the Holy Scriptures during the worship services.

LITURGY—From the Greek *leitourgia*, public service. A collection of prayers, readings, litanies, authorized for use in services of worship, administration of sacraments, and other ceremonial usage. The word is sometimes used by liturgists in the narrower sense of the ritual of Holy Communion.

MENSA—From the Latin *mensa*, a table. The top of the altar.

NARTHEX—The portion of the church containing the vestibule at the main entrance.

NAVE—From the Latin *navis*, a ship. The main part of the church between the principal entrance and the chancel. A good many early Christian churches were shaped somewhat like a ship of those times.

OFFICE LIGHTS—An inexact term usually given to branched lights when used on the altar. In contradistinction to eucharistic lights, the office lights are supposed to be used at minor, nonsacramental services, or "offices."

PARAMENTS—From the Latin *parare*, to prepare. The hangings or linens used in the sanctuary proper.

PRIE-DIEU—French, meaning pray God. A bench for kneeling at prayer.

PULPIT—From the Latin *pulpitum*, a stage or platform. The desk from which sermons are preached.

RABATO or REBATO—From the French *rabat*, from *rabattre*, to beat down. A stiff, turned-back collar holding a vestee in place. The rabato, although worn exclusively by clergymen in modern times, is not an ecclesiastical vestment in the strict sense.

REREDOS—From the Anglo-French *rere*, rear; and *dos*, back. The ornamental screen at the back of an altar.

RETABLE—A ledge or shelf above and at the back of the altar. On this shelf the cross and candles are placed. *See* GRADIN.

ROBE—A black garment worn by ministers during the worship and ceremonial services of the church. The word "robe" is preferable to "gown" which properly belongs to academic functions.

RUBRICS—Rules or directions indicating how worship, ceremonies, or rites are to to performed. Instructions regarding liturgical action. Formerly, such directions were printed in red ink; hence, the name. Some Protestant ministers misuse this term as if it meant prayers.

SANCTUARY—From the Latin *sanctuarium*, holy place. The part of the chancel of a church in which the altar is placed. In some churches it is separated from the remainder of the chancel by a railing.

STOLE—From the Greek *stole*, a garment. A narrow band of fine cloth worn around the neck of a minister. The ends reach near the knees. Its symbolic significance as a vestment is uncertain. Basically it signifies submission, obedience.

SUPERFRONTAL—Often called a FRONTLET. The altar hanging which extends the entire length of the altar and falls six or seven inches below the edge of the mensa.

SURPLICE—From the Latin *super*, over; and *pelliceae*, skin. The white linen garment worn over the fur or skin garment which was used in medieval times for protection of the clergy from cold during church and chapel services. In modern usage in the distinctively liturgical churches it is simply a white linen vestment, usually worn over a cassock.

VESTMENTS—From the Latin *vestimentum*, a garment. Garments used by ministers, choristers, and organists in church during worship services. The word is sometimes applied also to altar hangings.

WAFER—Unleavened bread in very thin, round pieces. Now frequently used in the administration of Holy Communion as a substitute for small cubes of ordinary white bread.

WINE—The fermented juice of the grape, used by the distinctively liturgical churches as one of the elements in the Lord's Supper. In the free churches the unfermented juice of the grape, with a preservative, is preferred.

Bibliography

Arnett, Clark, Stewart. *Methodist Altars.* Privately published by Mrs. B. B. Arnett, 2009 East Washington St., Orlando, Fla.

Bailey, Albert Edward, ed., *The Arts and Religion.* New York: The Macmillan Co., 1944.

Conover, Elbert M. *Building for Worship.* New York: Interdenominational Bureau of Church Architecture, 1945.

Gibson, George M. *The Story of the Christian Year.* New York and Nashville: Abingdon Press, 1945.

Leach, William H. *Protestant Church Building.* New York and Nashville: Abingdon Press, 1948.

——. *The Use of Candles in Christian Fellowship.* New York: Goodenough & Woglom Co., 1940.

McClinton, K. K. *Flower Arrangement in the Church.* New York: Morehouse-Gorham Co., 1944.

McClinton, K. K., and Squier, I. W. *Good Housekeeping in the Church.* New York: Morehouse-Gorham Co., 1951.

Menges, David A. *The Altar Guild.* Philadelphia: Muhlenberg Press, 1944.

Palmer, Albert W. *Come, Let Us Worship.* New York: The Macmillan Co., 1941.

Ritter, Richard H. *The Arts of the Church.* Boston: Pilgrim Press, 1947.

Scotford, John R. *The Church Beautiful.* Boston: Pilgrim Press, 1945.

Smart, Henry, comp., *The Altar, Its Ornaments and Its Care.* New York: Morehouse-Gorham Co., 1925.

Stafford, Thomas A. *Christian Symbolism in the Evangelical Churches.* New York and Nashville: Abingdon Press, 1942.

Strodach, Paul Z. *A Manual on Worship.* Philadelphia: Muhlenberg Press, 1930.

Index